D1518645

Abortion

Critical World Issues

CRITICAL WORLD ISSUES

Abortion

Mike Walters

MASON CREST
PHILADELPHIA

Mason Crest
450 Parkway Drive, Suite D
Broomall, PA 19008
www.masoncrest.com

Printed and bound in the United States of America.

CPSIA Compliance Information: Batch #CWI2016.
For further information, contact Mason Crest at 1-866-MCP-Book.

First printing
1 3 5 7 9 8 6 4 2

Library of Congress Cataloging-in-Publication Data

    on file at the Library of Congress
      ISBN: 978-1-4222-3646-8 (hc)
      ISBN: 978-1-4222-8126-0 (ebook)

Critical World Issues series ISBN: 978-1-4222-3645-1

Table of Contents

KEY ICONS TO LOOK FOR:

Words to Understand: These words with their easy-to-understand definitions will increase the reader's understanding of the text, while building vocabulary skills.

Sidebars: This boxed material within the main text allows readers to build knowledge, gain insights, explore possibilities, and broaden their perspectives by weaving together additional information to provide realistic and holistic perspectives.

Research Projects: Readers are pointed toward areas of further inquiry connected to each chapter. Suggestions are provided for projects that encourage deeper research and analysis.

Text-Dependent Questions: These questions send the reader back to the text for more careful attention to the evidence presented there.

Series Glossary of Key Terms: This back-of-the book glossary contains terminology used throughout this series. Words found here increase the reader's ability to read and comprehend higher-level books and articles in this field.

Basics of Abortion

K arla (name changed for *confidentiality* purposes) was a 14-year-old girl who lived in the Republic of Ireland. She was raped by the father of one of her school friends and became pregnant. The Irish constitution forbids *abortion*, but every year, thousands of Irish women travel to the United Kingdom (UK), where abortions became legal in 1967.

Karla's Story

Karla pleaded with her parents to take her to London for an abortion, and they granted her request. Because of the ongoing rape trial of her school friend's father, Karla's family told the Irish police about their plans to travel to the London. This resulted in a legal uproar in Ireland, and the case, taken up by

A public demonstration against abortion outside the capital building in Topeka, Kansas. Abortion is a very controversial issue in the United States and elsewhere.

the media, was broadcast nationally and internationally.

Many people felt that the girl should be allowed to have an abortion in spite of the laws prohibiting it. Because she had been raped, they argued, an exception should be made. Lawyers, however, continued to argue the case in court. Eventually, the Irish High Court ruled that Karla had no legal right to end her pregnancy. Instead, they decided that the rights of her unborn baby had to be protected.

The Irish police telephoned the girl's family in London and

 Words to Understand in This Chapter

abortion—the termination of a pregnancy with the death of the embryo or fetus.

conception—the process of becoming pregnant involving fertilization or implantation or both.

confidential—secret or private.

contraception—things that are done to prevent a woman from becoming pregnant.

embryo—the developing human individual from the time of implantation to the end of the eighth week after conception.

fetus—a developing human from usually eight weeks after conception to birth.

gestation—the time when a person is developing inside its mother before it is born; also, the process of development that happens during this time.

induce—to cause something to happen.

miscarriage—a condition in which a pregnancy ends too early—especially between the 12th and 28th week of gestation—and does not result in the birth of a live baby.

pro-choice—believing that pregnant women should have the right to choose to have an abortion.

pro-life—opposed to abortion.

Pregnant women have to deal with a great many issues in deciding whether to progress with or terminate a pregnancy.

demanded that they return to Ireland without having the abortion. By this point, Karla was extremely distressed and contemplating suicide. There was a wave of national and international public protest and sympathy on her behalf. Huge crowds marched through the streets, showing their support for Karla and calling for a change in the Irish abortion laws.

Finally, after several difficult weeks, the court ruled that Karla could have an abortion in London because her suicide threats proved that her life was in danger. However, the court also made it clear that Karla's case did not change Ireland's laws. Abortion was still illegal there, except to save a woman's life, and it remains so today.

Abortion Defined

Abortion is the ending of a pregnancy due to the death of the *embryo* or *fetus* in the mother's womb. An abortion can occur naturally in what is known as a *miscarriage* or "spontaneous abortion." It can also be *induced* by controlled medical treatment or by illegal "back-street" and homemade procedures.

Every day, women throughout the world actively seek an abortion as a way of ending a pregnancy. What leads them to

The arrival of a newborn baby can be a happy time, but it can also be a problematic period for a new mother.

decide that abortion is the best option? How emotionally painful is this decision for a woman? The reasons for abortion are diverse, as we will discover later in the book.

Questions about Abortion

According to the Guttmacher Institute's 2008 study, there are an estimated 43.8 million abortions performed worldwide every year. This compares to an estimated 131.4 million births per year—a ratio of one abortion for every three live births. The World Health Organization (WHO) reported 21.6 million women experience an unsafe, often illegal, abortion in the world each year, with 86 percent of these in developing countries.

Why do so many women throughout the world resort to a criminal act that risks their health in order to terminate a pregnancy? What kind of health risks are involved? We will look at

 Abortion Statistics Worldwide

With 2008 estimates of 22.2 million legal abortions and 21.6 million illegal, unsafe abortions each year, the approximate global monthly average is 3.65 million abortions. The proportion of abortions worldwide that take place in developing countries increased from 78 percent to 86 percent between 1995 and 2008, in part because the proportion of all women who live in developing countries increased during this period.

Abortion Around the World

The situation regarding abortion differs in various countries around the world because of factors such as access to education, religion, and wealth:

In the **Netherlands**, abortion rates are relatively very low because women can get cheap, safe contraception and receive comprehensive sex education in school. In 2008 (the most recent year for which global data on abortion is available), there were 27,600 abortions in the Netherlands, or 8 per 1,000 women aged 15 to 44.

Brazil is the world's most populous Roman Catholic country, with about 140 million people. In Brazil, abortion is illegal except in cases where a child was conceived after a rape, when the mother's life is in danger, or when the fetus has severe genetic abnormalities. Although exact numbers are impossible to determine, experts estimate that Brazilian women undergo an estimated 500,000 to 1 million abortions every year. Although most abortions are illegal, prosecution for this crime is relatively rare.

Zambia was the first country in Africa south of the Sahara Desert to make abortions legal, but the country is so poor that there are not enough doctors to perform them. As a result, safe and sanitary abortions are inaccessible to many women, who often resort to illegal abortions in conditions that are more likely to result in the mother's death.

the cases of abortion in countries that prohibit the practice as well as other cases in parts of the world that tolerate abortion. Some statistics are surprising: why, for example, is the abortion rate generally lower in countries where it is practiced legally?

Even in countries where abortion is legal, people's opinions on the practice are divided. For example, some *pro-life* groups believe that life begins at *conception*, the very start of a pregnancy, and that, therefore, abortion is a form of murder. The opposing argument from *pro-choice* campaigners is that a pregnant woman's right to choose whether or not to have an abortion should be respected. Who should have the final decision:

People hold anti-abortion signs at a rally protesting legislation in North Carolina that would require a longer waiting period for women seeking an abortion.

society, doctors, or the woman herself? Should the unborn fetus's right to life be the most important factor? These issues will be discussed in the following chapters.

We will also look at how advances in medical science and embryology affect abortion practice and learn the course of abortion legislation throughout history to the present day. There are also moral and ethical questions surrounding abortion in the light of medical and religious contexts, as well as social and economic factors in different cultures which need to be examined.

Beginnings of Abortion

The practice of abortion has existed since ancient times. The Assyrians and Babylonians, who lived 4,000 years ago in the Middle East, punished women who had abortions. In ancient Israel, anyone who assisted a woman in aborting her fetus was considered a criminal. In early Egypt, however, abortion was not against the law.

There are medical texts dating from 1300 BCE that record concoctions of herbs, spices, and animal dung that were used by women as *contraceptives* and to induce an abortion. Ancient Greek and Roman texts over 2,000 years old also show evidence of powerful drugs and violent exercises being used by women as a means of aborting a fetus.

The ancient Greek philosopher Aristotle (384-322 BCE) taught that a fetus originally has a vegetable soul. This evolves into an animal soul during the early stages of pregnancy before finally becoming animated, or brought to life, with a human soul. This belief was called delayed ensoulment and was wide-

Hippocrates

The ancient Greek doctor Hippocrates (460-377 BCE) is often called the Father of Medicine. An oath attributed to him is still taken by many doctors today. There are different versions, but the classic Hippocratic Oath includes concepts such as putting the good of patients above the interests of doctors and emphasizes a doctor's role in striving to preserve life. His oath taught that it was wrong to give medicine to induce an abortion: "I will neither give a deadly drug to anybody who asked for it, nor will I make a suggestion to this effect. Similarly I will not give to a woman an abortive remedy. In purity and holiness I will guard my life and my art."

ly accepted at the time. It was believed to occur at 40 days after conception for male fetuses and 90 days after conception for females. So abortion was not condemned if it was performed early in *gestation*, the period when the fetus develops in the womb. But if an abortion was done later in pregnancy, then people believed a human soul had been destroyed.

Religious Attitudes on Abortion

Islamic beliefs on the life of an unborn child have varied throughout history. Traditionally, Muslims have believed that a

Memorial headstone to "Victims of Abortion" at a Roman Catholic church.

fetus becomes a person before birth, but there has not always been agreement on when exactly this occurs. Some medieval authorities recorded it as happening at 120 days of gestation, after which abortion was considered an act of murder.

The early Hebrew belief was that the fetus did not have the same moral status as a person who was born, so human life was only achieved at birth. Later, however, embryonic and fetal life were more valued, and abortion was permitted only when the mother's physical health was at risk or in cases of serious fetal abnormality. This has typically been the attitude toward abortion in Judaism, as well as in Christianity, which emerged from Judaism in the first century CE and adopted many of its scriptures and teachings.

Pro-Life Influences in the 19th Century

Eugenics is the belief that the human race can be improved through selective breeding and birth-control techniques. Supporters of eugenics surfaced in the 19th century with the likes of Francis Galton, a cousin of Charles Darwin who pioneered the eugenics movement in 1883. This movement sought to preserve a fit and healthy population not only by maintaining strict anti-abortion laws, but also by enforcing birth control and the sterilization of those deemed inferior, and therefore unfit, to reproduce.

The 19th century saw significant changes in attitudes toward abortion, resulting in new legislation and greater severity of punishments. In 1869, the Catholic Church under Pope Pius IX declared a total ban on abortion, proclaiming that life with a soul started at the moment of conception. Abortion was punished by excommunication, or exclusion from the church, the most severe penalty possible. In the United Kingdom and United States, strict anti-abortion laws were also passed, making abortion punishable by death in some cases.

In the mid-19th century, there was an effort to tighten abortion regulations, led, in part, by the medical community. By the late 1860s, uniform abortion prohibition had been established

 # Science and Religious Perspectives

In 1677, Antonie von Leeuwenhoek (right), a pioneer Dutch microscope maker, was the first person to observe moving sperm under a microscope. His discoveries led to a confused debate among scientists and theologians. If sperm were living organisms outside the womb, did life begin, therefore, at the moment of conception inside the womb? Scientific confusion was also caused when two 17th-century physicians—Thomas Fienus of Louvain, Belgium and Paolo Zacchia of Rome, Italy— claimed that a rational soul existed from the moment of conception after believing they saw fully-formed human shapes in early embryos while peering through primitive microscopes.

This dramatic illustration accompanied an 1867 magazine article, showing an illegal abortionist pushing a woman, who is dying from his malpractice, into a New York street.

The Abortionist and Seducer Thrusting their Dying Victim into the Street, at Lansingburg, N. Y.

in the United Kingdom and throughout most of the US. These laws would remain in place in all fifty US states until the 1960s. In the state of New Jersey, for example, the penalty for anybody assisting in an abortion ranged from fines—up to $5,000—to a 15-year prison sentence.

Effect on European Colonies

The new abortion intolerance extended to the European colonies in Asia, Africa, South America, and the Caribbean. For instance, Spain's strict anti-abortion laws were reflected in many of their South American colonies. Toward the end of the 19th century, China and Japan, which were under the influence of Western powers at the time, also criminalized abortion.

There was another motive behind the anti-abortion laws of the 19th century. The Western world was in the grip of the Industrial Revolution, and factories needed more and more workers to increase production. It was imperative, therefore, that women produce as many children as possible to increase the workforce. Unchecked, abortion would lead to a shortage of workers and subsequent economic disaster. European governments also needed a steady supply of people to work in their colonial lands.

Twentieth Century Shift toward Abortion

Though the legal position in the United States was against abortion, both rich and poor women continued to seek abortions illegally. Thousands died or were seriously injured due to unsanitary conditions and dangerous abortion methods.

During the 1950s and 1960s, the rise of the women's rights movement pushed the abortion debate to the forefront. Greater sexual freedom in the 1960s led to a further increase in illegal abortions. Abortion doctors often turned women away if they could not pay $1,000 or more in cash, which was a large sum at the time.

Pro-choice groups lobbied governments to loosen the laws on abortion. In the United States, women, inspired by the civil rights and antiwar movements, began to fight more actively for their rights. They marched and rallied for "abortion on demand." Similar demonstrations took place in the United Kingdom. The British government responded with the Abortion Act of 1967, which came into effect in 1968. This

A women's rights march in Washington, D.C., circa 1970. The women's rights movement of the 1960s and 1970s

allowed a pregnancy to be terminated under certain conditions and with the consent of two doctors.

Also in 1967, two American states, Colorado and California, introduced laws to legalize abortion for a very wide range of medical reasons. In 1970, the state of New York passed the first law allowing abortion on demand up to the 24th week of pregnancy. However, illegal abortion remained common since the laws were still restrictive for many women in other states.

An important piece of legislation in the United Kingdom was the Human Fertilization and Embryology Act of 1990.

This introduced a limit of 24 weeks into pregnancy for a legal abortion under certain circumstances and no limit for others. Before this change, a 28-week maximum had applied to all grounds for abortion.

Roe v. Wade

In 1973, Norma McCorvey—who went under the assumed name of Jane Roe—was a pregnant resident of Texas who challenged the constitutionality of the abortion laws in the state.

Since the landmark Roe v. Wade *case, pro-choice groups have challenged any proposed legislation that would reduce access to abortions for women.*

The laws at the time made it a crime for a woman to terminate her pregnancy except on medical advice to save the life of the mother. The defendant was county district attorney Henry Wade.

On January 22, 1973, the US Supreme Court ruled 7-2 that the Texas laws were unconstitutional under the Fourteenth Amendment, which protected the right to privacy. The ruling recognized that the right to privacy included a woman's choice to have an abortion throughout her pregnancy but balanced this against two interests of the state: protecting a woman's health and the potential for a new human life. The decision stated that until the end of the first three months of pregnancy,

Supreme Court Justice Harry Blackmun was responsible for writing the majority opinion in the Roe vs. Wade *case (1973), which legalized abortion in the United States.*

only a pregnant woman and her doctor have the legal right to make a decision about an abortion. After that point, it allowed state regulation of abortions. This ruling affected changes in the laws of forty-six states.

Reaction of Pro-Life Supporters

The *Roe vs. Wade* ruling energized the pro-life lobby. They began to demonstrate, using clinic blockades, legislative strategies, and legal challenges.

In response to the rise of pro-choice protests, an antiabortion movement formed protesting for the rights of the unborn child.

The first victory for pro-life campaigners came in July 1976, when Congress passed the Hyde Amendment. This banned government funding for an abortion through programs like Medicaid, unless a woman's life was in danger. After this was passed, many states stopped funding abortions unless they were considered medically necessary.

Though she was instrumental in making abortion legal in the United States, Norma McCorvey did not in fact have an abortion herself; she put her baby up for adoption. She has since changed her stance on the abortion debate, and in 1997, she started a pro-life outreach organization called Roe No More. In 2003, McCorvey filed a motion with the US District Court in Dallas to have the *Roe v. Wade* case overturned, presenting evidence that abortions hurt women, along with 1,000 signed statements by women saying they regretted their abortions. The court dismissed her motion the following year.

 # Text-Dependent Questions

1. Who led the pro-life campaign in the 19th century, and how far did this influence spread?
2. Name and explain two factors that led to a 20th-century shift toward abortion in the US.
3. Describe Norma McCorvey's case, what impact it had on the United States, and what her final position was years after the case.

 # Research Project

Using the Internet or your school library, research the topic of religious views on abortion, and answer the following question: "Should religion have a say in legal abortion issues?"

Some claim that the choice to have an abortion is a personal decision for a woman and should not be decided by the teachings of any organized religion, especially if she does not follow that particular faith. There should be "separation of church and state," where religions can influence only their followers' personal practices, while the government makes its policies for all citizens.

Others contend that religion should be able to affect the abortion debate because it is a moral issue concerning life and death. If, in fact, life begins at conception, many religions are calling for the protection of a person's life and preventing the killing of the innocent. Religions have guided the morality of societies for centuries and should be consulted in such a high-stakes matter.

Write a two-page report, using data you have found in your research to support your conclusion, and present it to your class.

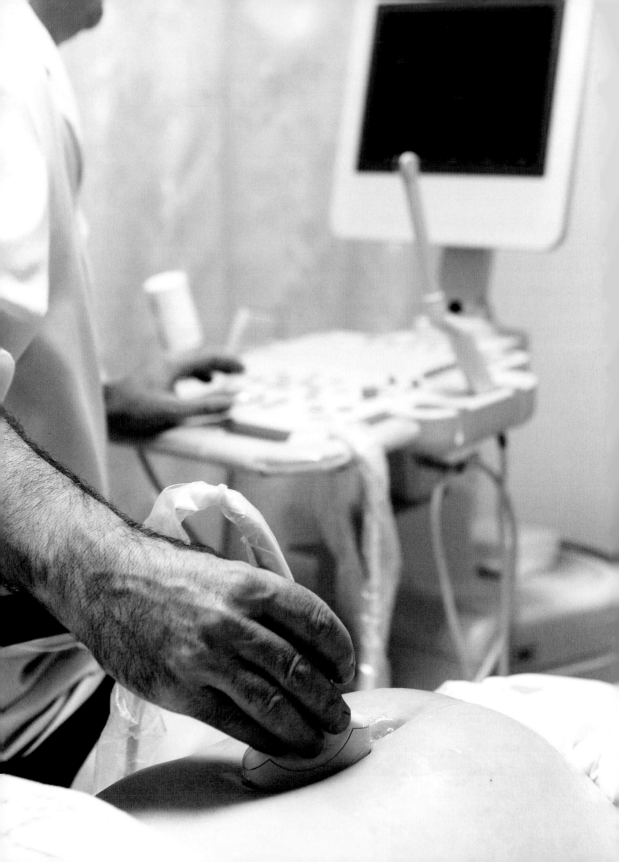

The Question of When Life Begins

The question of when life begins forms one of the central issues behind the abortion debate. Does life begin at conception, the very start of a pregnancy, or does it begin when the baby is born? Is it somewhere in between? In this chapter, we will examine the different stages of pregnancy and look at different views about when life begins.

A woman needs to conceive in order to get pregnant. Conception is a process involving three separate stages: *fertilization*, when male and female reproductive cells come together; division, when the new cell multiplies and creates more cells; and *implantation*, when the group of cells, known as an embryo, attaches itself to the wall of its mother's uterus).

From puberty, humans produce cells for reproduction. The male cells are sperm, stored in a man's testes; the female cells

Ultrasound technology uses sound waves to create an image of the embryo or fetus developing inside its mother's uterus. Ultrasounds provide a variety of information about how a pregnancy is progressing, and are often an element of prenatal care.

are eggs, stored in a woman's ovaries. Both the male and female sex cells contain the genetic information needed to make up the cells in a new human life. For fertilization to occur, a sperm and egg must join together. When a man and woman have sexual intercourse without using contraception, one sperm can fuse with a single egg. If fertilization does not occur, then the unfertilized egg is released from the woman's body, along with the built-up lining of the womb, in what is referred to as a period or menstruation. This occurs once every twenty-eight days or so.

Growth after Fertilization

As soon as an egg is fertilized, it starts to grow. It splits into two cells, which continue dividing to form a hollow cluster. After about five days, this lifeform grows tiny "fingers" around its outer edge, which burrow into the lining of a woman's uterus,

 Words to Understand in This Chapter

denomination—a religious organization whose congregations are united in their beliefs and practices.

fertilization—the joining of an egg cell and a sperm cell to form the first stage of an embryo.

implantation—the process of attachment of the early embryo to the maternal uterine wall.

sanctity—the quality or state of being holy, very important, or valuable.

trimester—a period of three months; especially one of three periods into which a woman's pregnancy is often divided.

The Process of Fertilization

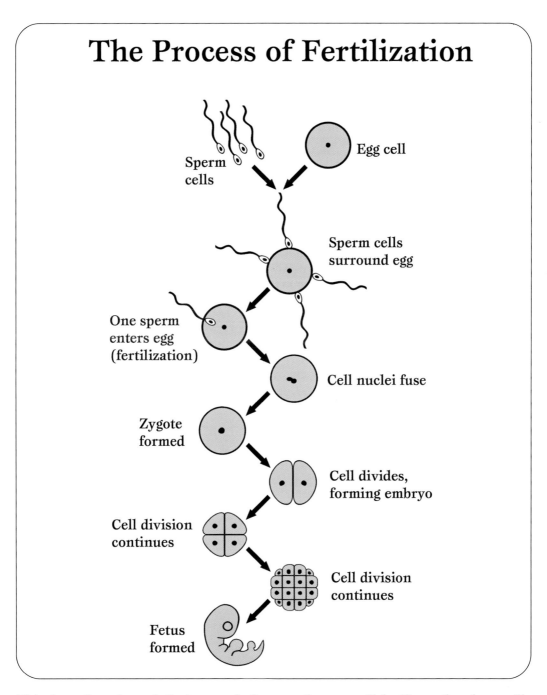

This chart shows how a baby is created when a male sperm cell fertilizes a female egg cell.

From Egg to Fetus

There are many different terms for cells formed during conception and pregnancy:

- An egg cell that has been fertilized by a sperm cell is called a zygote.
- A cluster of cells, formed when a zygote divides, is called a morula. This occurs roughly three days after fertilization.
- A morula forms into a hollow sphere called a blastocyst. This develops four to five days after fertilization.
- About a day later, the blastocyst implants into the lining of the uterus, now called an embryo until the eighth week.
- Approximately eight weeks after implantation, the embryo starts to look recognizably human. For the rest of the pregnancy, it is called a fetus.
- Once the fetus is born, it is called a baby.

or womb. This is called implantation. If the cluster of cells fails to implant in the uterus, it will not get the nutrients it needs and dies. But if implantation succeeds, the cluster feeds from the uterus's rich blood supply, and it grows very quickly. It develops into a minute creature, called an embryo, which is linked to the wall of the uterus by an umbilical cord and an organ called the placenta, a fluid-filled bag that provides surrounding protection.

Timing of Abortions

If a woman misses her period after sexual intercourse, there is a strong possibility that she has conceived and is pregnant.

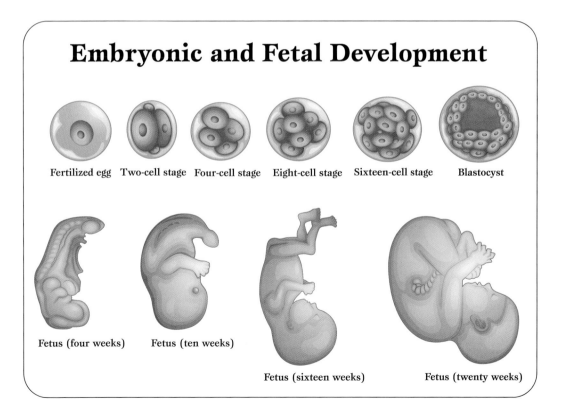

Embryonic and Fetal Development

Fertilized egg Two-cell stage Four-cell stage Eight-cell stage Sixteen-cell stage Blastocyst

Fetus (four weeks) Fetus (ten weeks) Fetus (sixteen weeks) Fetus (twenty weeks)

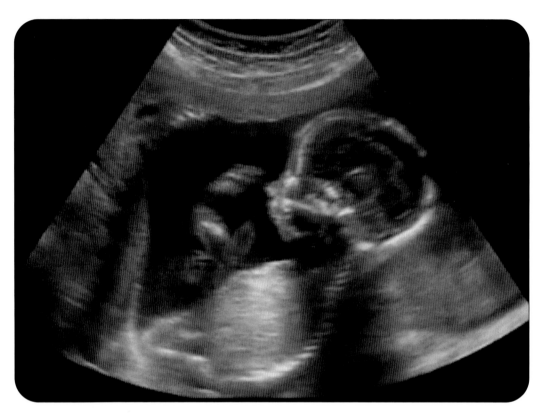

This image produced by ultrasound technology shows a four-month-old fetus.

Usually, she will take a home pregnancy test, followed by a pregnancy test at a clinic to confirm the result. A pregnancy is measured from the time of the woman's last period, and it takes approximately forty weeks from that point to the time of birth. The majority of abortions are carried out in the first twelve weeks of a pregnancy, called the first *trimester*, with very few occurring after twenty weeks. In the United Kingdom, for example, 91 percent of abortions are in the first twelve weeks of pregnancy, and 79 percent are in the first nine weeks. In the United States, 88.8 percent of all abortions occur within the first twelve weeks of pregnancy, 95 percent within fifteen weeks, and 98.6 percent within twenty weeks.

When Life Begins

Societies and organizations around the world hold different beliefs on the question of when life begins. Opinions range from the belief that life begins at the moment of fertilization to the view that life cannot be said to start until the child has been born. In between these two extremes are several stages where different groups believe a human being starts its existence.

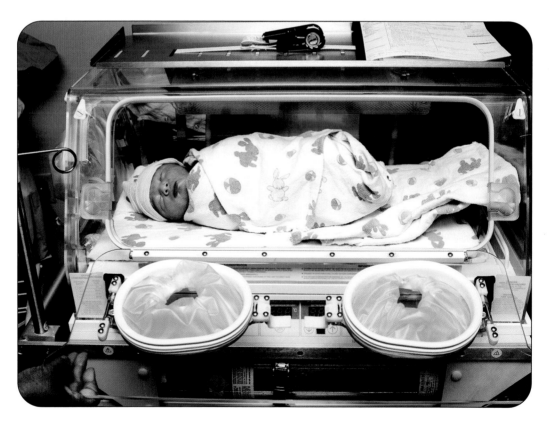

A premature baby in intensive care. Improvements in medical technology have shifted the time of viability, when the infant can survive outside the womb.

These crosses outside the St. Bartholomew Catholic Church in Columbus, Indiana, represent lives lost to abortion every hour.

These include "quickening," the time when the fetus first moves in the womb, or viability, when the fetus can survive outside the mother's womb.

Christian Perspectives

Christians are divided into two major groups: Catholics and Protestants. For the most part, both teach that human life begins at conception when the woman's egg is fertilized by a man's sperm. A unique, self-growing life begins at that moment, independent of the life of the mother and father. This is a human being with potential, not just a potential human being. The Christian view is that this life deserves the same the value, rights, and protection that are granted an infant, child, or adult. Christians maintain the Bible's teachings about life before birth. For them, God is both the creator and a sacred presence in a child growing in its mothers' womb.

Some Christian *denominations* also place paramount importance on the *sanctity* of all human life, including that of an unborn child, but they also permit abortion in exceptional cases, such as when the pregnancy threatens the life of the mother.

Buddhist Beliefs

The early scriptures of Buddhism teach that human life starts with conception. If this is so, then an abortion is seen as morally wrong because it breaks one of the basic laws of Buddhism, which is to abstain from harming or killing living beings. Some branches of Buddhism, however, tolerate abortion under certain circumstances.

In the spring of 2016, the US Supreme Court heard arguments about a controversial Texas law that regulated abortions. Critics of the 2013 law claimed that it had required abortion clinics to make expensive changes in the way they operated, causing more than half of the state's clinics to close. Supporters of the law said that the changes were required to make them safer.

Other Religious Stances

In Hindu tradition and philosophy, abortion is forbidden except when the life of the mother is threatened. The Hindu faith believes that the soul enters the womb at the time of conception. Abortion is called garbha batta, "womb killing," or brhoona hathya, meaning "killing the undeveloped soul."

Judaism teaches that life begins at birth, although abortion is still discouraged besides when the mother's life is at risk.

The fetus has great value because it is potentially a human life, but it will only gain full human status at birth.

In Islamic teaching, a soul enters the fetus not at the moment of conception, but at 120 days after. Thus, abortion is permitted after 120 days only to save the mother's life. Before that point, there are different schools of thought, but most permit abortion if the child has a physical or mental defect that would cause suffering.

 # Text-Dependent Questions

1. Describe the growth process from fertilization to the development of an embryo.
2. Explain the beliefs of three religions with different views on when human life begins.

 # Research Project

Using the Internet or your school library, research the topic of when human life begins, and answer the following question: "Does human life begin at conception?"

Some believe a human life technically begins at the point of conception and should therefore be granted the right to be born without interference. From this point on, the life develops on its own, multiplying its cells and forming specific body parts, including the brain, heart, and face. It is without a doubt a living being that is human, so who can say that human life has not begun at this point? If we deny that it is a human life, we risk the danger of judging worth by ability, where babies are not as fully human as adults, or people with disabilities are not as valuable as typical people.

Others argue that a developing embryo is simply a mass of living cells. It can only be considered a full human life when it is born or at least when it is further developed. Until there is an ability to think and feel, which happens later in pregnancy, it is not yet a life. At fertilization and the early stages of growth, the mother should be able to have an abortion because the embryo or fetus is not a fully human life.

Write a two-page report, using data you have found in your research to support your conclusion, and present it to your class.

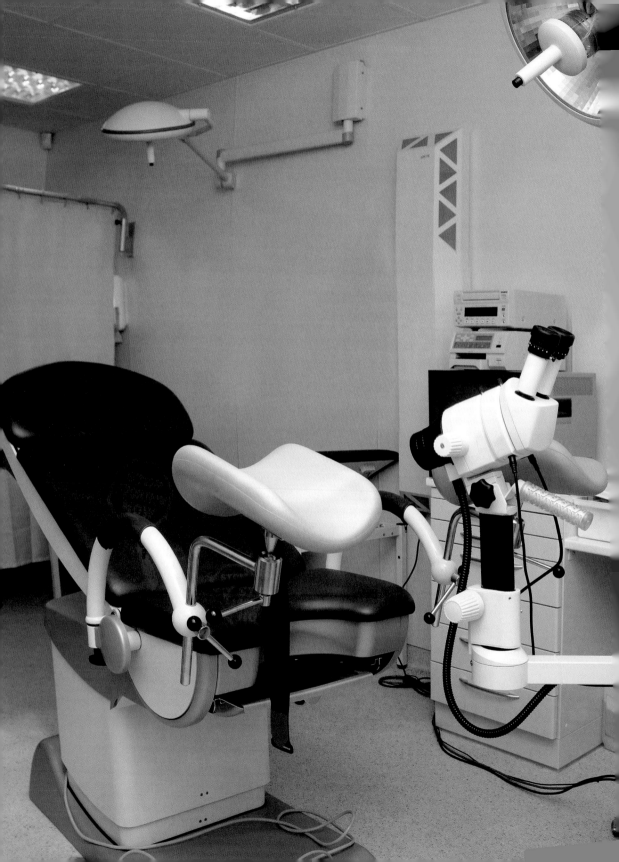

Abortion Procedures

T here are several procedures available for deliberately ending a pregnancy. Women can have a medical abortion, with drugs, or a surgical one. Although these are normally straightforward methods, some people are concerned about the possible physical, psychological, and emotional effects.

Early Abortions

An abortion can happen naturally in a miscarriage, or it can be induced deliberately. There are several different abortion procedures, depending on the stage of the pregnancy. In early medical abortion, up to nine weeks, drugs are used. The regime of drugs differs from one country to another.

In the United States, the two drugs used are methotrexate

Legal abortions are carried out in sterile facilities, such as this one, by trained professionals.

and misoprostol. Methotrexate is given by injection and stops the embryo's cells from dividing, thereby preventing further development. Misoprostol is then inserted into the vagina, often by the woman at home, five to seven days after the methotrexate injection. This drug causes the womb to contract. The woman experiences cramping and bleeding and the embryo is usually expelled within a week.

Methods for Later Stages

From about weeks five to twelve of a pregnancy, a method called "vacuum" or "suction aspiration" can be used; it is the most common type of abortion performed. A woman can sometimes choose to have this under a *local anesthetic* or a *general anesthetic.* During a vacuum aspiration abortion, a thin tube is eased into the uterus through the cervix (the passage that links the vagina to the womb). By using a pump, the contents of the uterus pass out of the womb and into the tube.

For a longer gestation, usually from weeks fifteen to nineteen, a surgical procedure known as "dilation and evacuation"

 Words to Understand in This Chapter

congenital—existing at or dating from birth.

general anesthetic—a drug that makes a person unconscious and unable to feel pain.

hygienic—relating to being clean and the things that are done to maintain good health: of or relating to hygiene.

local anesthetic—a drug that makes a part of the body unable to feel pain.

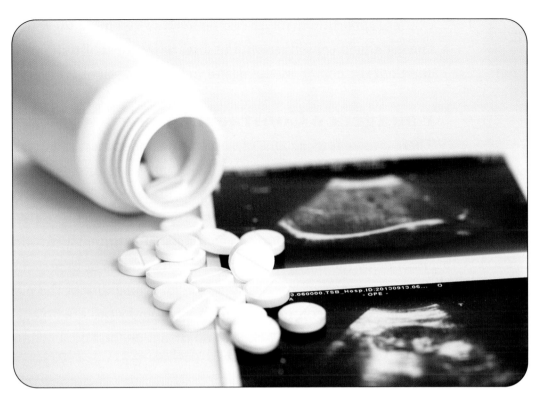

The drug RU-486 or mifepristone, is marketed under the name Mifeprex. It works by blocking a hormone called progesterone that is needed for a pregnancy to continue.

is used. At this stage the fetus is too large to remove by suction without causing harm to the mother. The woman is given a general anesthetic, and for procedures later in the second trimester, a shot may be given through the woman's abdomen to stop the heart of the fetus. The doctor then stretches the passage through the cervix. When it is wide enough, forceps are used to remove most of the fetus. A vacuum pump is then used to clear out any remaining tissue or body parts.

Between weeks twenty and twenty-four, a surgical two-stage abortion or a medical induction is used. A surgical two-stage abortion involves two operations to remove the fetus. During a medical induction, the fetal heart is usually stopped, and then the doctor uses drugs to induce early labor.

Emergency Contraceptives

There are a few means of preventing pregnancy after sex unprotected by contraceptives. The "morning after pill" is offered to women as an emergency contraceptive. It is, in fact, a series of pills and one of the few forms of contraception that can be taken—up to three to five days after intercourse—to either delay the release of an egg from the ovaries or to prevent the implantation of a fertilized egg. The availability of the pill has caused deep controversy and is opposed by pro-life organizations, which see it as a quick and casual method of abortion

Plan B is an example of a form of emergency contraceptive known as the "morning after pill." It contains a hormone called levonorgestrel, which can prevent fertilization of an egg.

because its effect can occur after fertilization, when they believe a human life has already begun.

Dangers of Abortion

Legal abortions are usually very safe when performed by trained medical staff in *hygienic* surroundings. The risks increase the longer a woman is into her pregnancy. In the first trimester, the Guttmacher Institute reports legal abortions in the United States have virtually no chance of long-term consequences such as infertility. The risk of death is 1 in a million in the first eight weeks, 1 per 29,000 at sixteen to twenty weeks, and 1 per 11,000 at twenty-one weeks or later.

More common are minor complications that occur during the procedure. A woman may experience an infection, incomplete abortion, or heavy bleeding after an abortion. Bacterial infections happen in less than one percent of cases of vacuum aspirations but may be slightly higher the later it is into pregnancy. Antibiotics are used to treat the infection, and very rarely, a repeat suction or surgery may be required. Incomplete abortions also happen less than one percent of the time. In such instances, fetal tissue or other products from pregnancy are not completely removed from the uterus, leading to heavy or irregular bleeding or infection. It is treated with a repeated procedure of removing tissue from the uterus.

Unsafe Abortion Statistics

The World Health Organization (WHO) states that 21.6 million women worldwide had an unsafe abortion in 2008, with 18.5 million of these in developing countries. The number of women who die from complications of unsafe abortions annually is estimated to be 47,000. This means that up to 13 percent of all maternal deaths are due to unsafe abortions.

In developed regions, there are 0.7 deaths of women in unsafe abortions per 100,000 live births, but in Eastern Africa, the figure is 100 deaths per 100,000 live births—this means the chance of a woman dying in this way is 142 times greater in Eastern Africa than in a developed country.

In South Central Asia, Southeastern Asia, and Western Asia, 60 to 65 percent of abortions were unsafe. Poor Pakistani women commonly use unsafe methods and untrained providers, leading to 45 percent having complications from an abortion, compared to 31 percent for wealthier Pakistani women.

Rates for Illegal Abortions

The Guttmacher Institute stated 40 percent of the world's 1.55 billion women of reproductive age (15 to 44) live in countries where abortion is illegal or highly restricted, virtually all in the developing world. In Africa, 92 percent of women of reproductive age live under severely restrictive laws; in Latin America, 97 percent do.

In Uganda, about 300,000 abortions take place each year despite the fact that abortion is legal only to save a woman's life. These are unsafe abortions because they are done in unhygienic conditions without trained professionals. Unsafe abortions in Uganda are a leading cause of pregnancy-related death. At the current pace, half of all Ugandan women will require treatment for complications related to abortion at some point in their lives.

Illegal Abortions in Brazil

In Brazil, abortion is illegal except in cases of rape, when the mother's life is in danger, and in rare instances of anencephaly, where the fetus lacks part of the brain and cannot survive. Outside of these reasons, women who have abortions are subject to one to three years in prison, while doctors can get twenty years. Still, a million abortions are performed in Brazil annually, and 200,000 women are hospitalized for complications, including infections and vaginal bleeding.

Many women use misoprostol at home to end their pregnancies, but without proper medical guidance, it can be ineffective and dangerous, potentially causing a rupture of the uterus or severe bleeding. The risk of complications using the drug increase after the first nine weeks of pregnancy, but women in Brazil often wait before seeking an abortion because of the social consequences and financial cost. Since the drug is not legally sold in Brazil, there is a real risk that the instructions are mislabeled, or the drugs being sold are actually sugar pills or some other dangerous medication that fails to safely terminate a pregnancy.

In some countries, such as Argentina, Brazil, Colombia, the Dominican Republic, Indonesia, Nigeria, Philippines, Spain, and South Africa, misoprostol is readily available on the black market. In most of these countries, women cannot obtain legal abortions. They buy the medication in order to terminate their pregnancies secretly, without medical help. The drug can often be purchased very cheaply, requiring no prescription.

Ugandan women line up at the Kanungu Health Center to receive HIV and cervical cancer counselling and testing, and to learn more about available family planning services.

Emotional Consequences

The psychological and emotional effects of having an abortion can vary greatly from woman to woman. A decision to end a pregnancy is not always an easy one to make, and the woman may feel a certain degree of sadness even if she sees the abortion as necessary. The feelings experienced after an abortion can range from sheer relief and liberation to a deep, inexpressible grief and regret. Studies in the United Kingdom have shown that about three percent of women harbor long-term feelings of loss and guilt, some feeling that the abortion was a mistake.

Consideration should be given to the women who wanted to continue their pregnancy but, due to a malformation or *congenital* defect in the fetus, had to undergo a termination. A late-term abortion in these circumstances can add significantly to a woman's distress.

Some women may feel they need to talk to a post-abortion counselor. This can help them to fully acknowledge any feelings of loss they have, and although they may feel very emotional after an abortion, the counseling can be extremely therapeutic. Feelings of anger can also emerge, directed at themselves or perhaps at their partners, and relationships may break up after an abortion.

Many pro-life groups believe that a large percentage of women who have undergone an abortion experience serious depression and massive feelings of guilt. This has been called Posttraumatic Abortion Syndrome, Post Abortion Syndrome, or PAS. Every woman reacts in a different way. They each have different responses in different time frames. Some women repress or are unaware of any aftereffects for many years. Studies in the United States report negative reactions to include feelings of guilt, shame, anxiety, helplessness, grief, and remorse.

Positive Feelings from Abortion

Abortion can produce positive reactions too. Some women feel more in control of their lives following an abortion. They may feel stronger, more determined, and more assertive. An abor-

Offering for the Unborn

In Japan, some women who have had abortions make offerings to Buddha statues that represent "Jizo," the "Buddha of aborted babies." This way, a woman can alleviate some of the guilt or remorse she feels and be comforted that the Buddha will take care of the unborn babies in the afterlife.

Jizo statues at a temple in Tokyo. Those who have had a miscarriage, stillbirth, or abortion decorate the statues in honor of the unborn child.

tion sometimes leaves women feeling more certain that she wants a child, but at the right time in the future. She may also make a decision to practice safer sex and be more aware of her bodily changes as well as her emotional and physical needs. A Canadian survey was done of women who had recently chosen to terminate their first pregnancy at an early stage. It found that almost 80 percent "felt relief and satisfaction" soon after they had had the abortion.

 ## Text-Dependent Questions

1. What are three different types of abortion procedures performed at different points of a pregnancy?
2. Provide two unsafe aspects of illegal abortions.
3. Give two negative and two positive emotions experienced by women after an abortion.

 ## Research Project

Using the Internet or your school library, research the topic of fathers and abortions, and answer the following question: "Should the baby's father have a say on whether or not an abortion is done?"

Some think that the father should influence the decision because the fetus is as much his as it is the mother's. If the child were born, the father would be one of the two parents who could make legal choices about the child's life, so he should have a say in the fetus's life in the womb, whether for or against abortion. The father also has emotions and can be affected, especially if he believes it is a human life from conception.

Others say is the father should not have influence over on an abortion decision because it is the woman's body and her life that would be disrupted, not the man's. The woman has to endure the health risks and lifestyle changes that come with abortion or carrying a baby to birth, so it should be her decision alone.

Write a two-page report, using data you have found in your research to support your conclusion, and present it to your class.

SYNDROME

POST

VORTEMENT

parlons en!

Reasons for an Abortion

T here are many reasons why women choose to have an abortion. Faced with an unwanted pregnancy, a woman may feel she is too young or too old to have a baby. Some women simply do not want children or do not want to increase their family size. Others have an abortion because of medical risks to themselves or because of a serious fetal genetic disorder. The reasons given are both complex and varied, especially in context of different regions of the world.

Intended and Unintended Pregnancies

Data from 2012 shows that of the 213 million pregnancies worldwide, 60 percent were intended. Of the 40 percent that were unintended, 50 percent resulted in abortion, 13 percent

People protest against abortion in France on the eve of a parliamentary debate on legislation that would make it easier to terminate a pregnancy. The legislation passed in August 2014, allowing women to have an abortion for any reason so long as they were no more than twelve weeks pregnant. Previously, abortions were only allowed in cases of medical emergency.

in miscarriage, and 38 percent in birth. In the United States, 45 percent of pregnancies were unintended—2.1 million total. Excluding miscarriages, 42 percent of these ended in abortion, and 58 percent ended in birth.

Nonmedical Reasons for Abortion

Worldwide, 60.8 percent of women are legally able to obtain abortions for reasons not related to health. Some countries, such as Afghanistan, Indonesia, and Iran, prohibit abortion except for cases where the mother's life is endangered by the pregnancy. In countries such as the United States, United Kingdom, and Scandinavian nations—where abortion is obtainable to any woman who wants it—around 90 percent of abortions take place for *socioeconomic* reasons such as financial well-being. Some 73 percent of US women feel that they lack the financial resources to have a baby, one of the most common reasons for abortion.

Many women who decide to have an abortion say they do so because they are not ready for the responsibility of bringing

 Words to Understand in This Chapter

Down Syndrome—a congenital condition characterized by moderate to severe mental impairment, slanting eyes, a broad short skull, broad hands with short fingers, and trisomy of the human chromosome numbered 21.

mortality rate—the number of a particular group who die each year.

socioeconomic—of, relating to, or involving a combination of social and economic factors.

A teenager who finds out that she is pregnant may want to terminate a pregnancy because she feels that she is too young to have a baby.

up a child, or they do not wish to have a baby at all. Seventy-four percent of women having abortions in the United States say that having a baby would interfere with work, school, or the ability to care for other children. A woman may already be committed to looking after a sick partner or elderly parents and feel that it is impossible to commit to the demands of a new baby as well.

A small minority of all abortions are sought because of an abusive sexual act. In the United States, 1 percent of pregnant women indicate they want an abortion because they had been

A woman who is struggling to bring up a large family may not want to have another child.

rape victims, and 0.5 percent say they want to end a pregnancy due to incest.

The Role of the Partner

Forty-eight percent of women in the United States who wanted an abortion said they did not want to be a single parent or were having relationship problems with their husband or partner. Many times, a woman is unsure about whether or not the father will stay with her if she has their baby. If the father is not around, the woman may feel unable to cope with having a child on her own or feel that it is wrong to have a baby whose father will not be there to play an active role in bringing them up.

According to the laws in the majority of countries where abortion is legal, the father's consent to an abortion is not needed. Some men have felt frustrated that their feelings are not considered when making the decision. On the other hand, some women feel that the pregnancy and abortion only affect their body and that they alone should make such a choice. In societies that allow abortion on demand, however, many women want to discuss their pregnancy with the father of the fetus.

The Link between Contraception and Abortion

Contraceptive use around the world varies greatly. The United Nations documented that in 2015, 17 percent of married or in-

 Differing Reasons for Low Rates

In some Islamic countries, abortion rates are low because couples want to have large families, and there may be fewer unintended pregnancies because sex outside of marriage brings severe penalties for women. In the Netherlands, the abortion rate is low for completely different reasons: though Dutch women prefer small families, and sex outside of marriage is common, widespread use of effective contraception makes abortion uncommon.

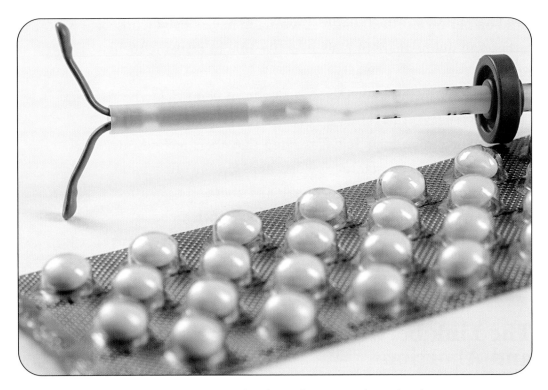

The use of contraceptives, such as these, has been shown to reduce abortion rates.

union women in Western African countries used contraception, compared to 82 percent in East Asia. Recent studies have shown that generally, abortion rates are highest in societies where there is a desire for smaller families, where effective birth control methods are not practiced, and where induced abortion is relied on for birth control.

Family-planning programs in many developing countries have helped to increase access to contraceptive services. This has led to fewer unwanted pregnancies and a subsequent reduction in abortion rates. However, in countries where abortion is illegal and birth control inadequate, there are still high abortion rates, with correspondingly high *mortality rates*. Worldwide in 2014, there were 59,178 unsafe abortions a day, 86 percent of which were in developing countries, causing the deaths of at 129 women each day. Some 81 percent of unintended pregnancies in developing countries occur among women who do not have access to modern contraception—many of these cases result in unsafe abortions.

Medical Reasons for Abortion

Sometimes, a pregnant woman finds herself in circumstances that limit or take away her freedom to choose. She might be very ill, perhaps through an accident, and an abortion may be necessary to save her life. Other conditions which might threaten the health of the woman include severe heart and kidney disease.

Through ultrasound scans, a pregnant woman may learn from the doctor that her fetus is so damaged it would not survive birth, in which case the woman may choose an abortion. In other situations, a woman may be told that her fetus will be born with serious physical or mental impairment. She then has a very difficult decision to make—to abort the fetus or commit to the extra care necessary for the child's life.

Causes of Fetal Damage

The fetus can be harmed by exposure to infections, such as rubella (German measles), high radiation levels, alcohol or drugs, or high levels of toxic chemicals, including those found in some medicines. These substances can cause the fetus serious damage.

One legal drug that caused great controversy in the early days of the abortion debate was thalidomide. Thalidomide was prescribed as a sedative and to relieve morning sickness in pregnant women. However, it was found to cause severe birth defects in infants. There were several high-profile cases of women who had taken thalidomide and then opted to abort the damaged fetus, including that of Sheri Finkbine, who had to travel from her home in the United States to Sweden in 1962 in order to have an abortion. Other causes of fetal damage include genetic disorders, such as *Down Syndrome*, and inherited diseases.

The Case for People with Disabilities

The access to a legal abortion on the grounds of fetal abnormality, where the baby will be born with a disability of some kind, has raised serious concerns among many people, including pro-life supporters and disability-rights campaigners. These people believe that a child with a disability is fully human and can go on to lead a productive, happy life. While they may require extra assistance in certain areas from family, caregivers, or society, they can make a meaningful contribution to their communities and deserve the right to life. Those who help them may even learn greater compassion and sanctity of life in the process.

In December 2003, Joanna Jepson, a Church of England minister, questioned the abortion of a fetus with a cleft palate, which occurs when the cells of the lips, face, and palate fail to fuse together. The abortion had been carried out after the twenty-fourth week of the pregnancy, a time when, according to the UK Abortion Act, abortions are only allowed if a severe disability has been found in the fetus. In Jepson's opinion, the cleft palate did not amount to a serious disability.

 Text-Dependent Questions

1. Give at least three statistics regarding nonmedical reasons for abortions.
2. How is contraception related to unsafe abortions in the world?

 Research Project

Using the Internet or your school library, research the topic of fetal abnormalities and abortion, and answer the following question: "Should abortion be allowed for fetuses with abnormalities?"

Some contend that abortion should be allowed in these cases. If a mother wants to only bear children who can participate fully, both mentally and physically, in life, she should be able to make that choice. Why produce a distressing situation with a baby with special needs if you can prevent it? Some women may not have the financial means or emotional strength to care for a child with disabilities, and they should be able to have an abortion if they want.

Others argue that abortion should not be allowed for fetuses with disabilities. This is a sinister form of eugenics and no one should have the right to decide who is "normal" enough to be allowed to live. Everyone has imperfections and weaknesses, but they are not valued any less or given any less right to live because of them. The same is true of a life in the womb that may have physical or mental needs. Countless people with disabilities have led happy, successful lives, and some have made major impacts in the world. It is the duty of society to provide the necessary support and cherish each life as precious and meaningful.

Write a two-page report, using data you have found in your research to support your conclusion, and present it to your class.

5

Pro-Life and Pro-Choice Arguments

N ot everyone who has an opinion about abortion will take a definite pro-choice or pro-life view. However, their thoughts and feelings about abortion issues will undoubtedly be influenced by the arguments of these two opposing sides.

Those who advocate for the "right to choose" say that they should not be labeled "pro-abortion" and that their arguments concern women's rights over their own bodies. The pro-life supporters maintain that because human life begins at conception, all abortions involve the killing of innocent children. There are, however, developments that are complicating some of the issues.

Cells from fetuses that have been legally aborted are sometimes used in medical research that has saved many lives. For example, fetal tissue was used in the development of the polio vaccine and other lifesaving medicines. In the United States, strict federal guidelines control how fetal tissue can be collected and used. However, opponents of abortion have sometimes charged, inaccurately, that clinics such as Planned Parenthood are invested in encouraging people to have abortions because they profit from the illegal sale of fetal tissue to research hospitals.

Complicating Issues

The issue of fetal viability—the point at which a fetus can survive outside the mother's body—is a key point in opening up the debate to complex new questions.

In the last fifteen years or so, advances in medical technology have enabled women to give birth to very *premature* babies. A 2015 study by the *New England Journal of Medicine* showed a small number of babies born at twenty-two weeks were able to survive without major health problems after intensive medical treatment. While the vast majority born so prematurely (less than thirty-seven weeks) do not survive or have serious disabilities, the fact that a minority can survive without major health issues has forced people to reconsider the ethical issues surrounding late-term abortion.

The Pro-Choice Movement

Worldwide human rights laws protect pregnant women, but they do not automatically give them the right to have an abortion. Some women feel that they should be able to make that choice, and abortion should be available on demand with fewer

 Words to Understand in This Chapter

abortifacient—an agent, such as a drug, that induces abortion.

non-governmental organization—a voluntary group of individuals or organizations, not affiliated with any government and usually non-profit, that is formed to provide services or to advocate a public policy.

premature—born before the normal time.

Thousands gathered in Toronto to mark International Women Day with a protest march demanding improvements in many social issues.

legal restrictions, such as the need to refer to a second doctor. Women supporting the legalization of abortion call themselves the pro-choice movement.

Pro-choice supporters believe that abortion is not wrong in itself and should be far more widely available throughout the world. Contrary to the pro-life view, they tend not to acknowledge the fetus as a person, although they consider that from the embryonic stage on, there is "potential life." They argue, therefore, that because the fetus is not a person, it is not the rights of the fetus that are paramount, but those of the pregnant woman—she should have legal authority over what happens to her body. Supporters currently campaign for legalizing abortion in countries where there are high rates of dangerous illegal abortions. They also maintain that if contraception and education on birth-control were more widely available, far fewer abortions would happen worldwide.

Pro-Choice Arguments

Pro-choice supporters maintain that no one has a right to limit a woman's freedom of choice or her freedom of action. They do not see why women should tolerate intervention from government, religious organizations, friends, family, or members of the medical establishment on the question of whether or when they should be allowed to have an abortion. The pro-choice line of argument is that women have the right to control their own bodies. Supporters also feel that a pregnant woman should not have to justify her reasons in order to "win" an abortion.

In their support of legal abortion, pro-choice groups claim that the embryo or fetus does not have the same value as a born person. In the beginning, they say, the embryo is a collection of cells, not a person, and until a certain point, the fetus could not survive outside the womb. The woman, on the other hand, has conscious thought and is able to make practical and moral choices.

They also believe that a pregnant woman understands her own personal circumstances better than anyone else. They say she knows best how equipped she is to raise a child and into what conditions the child would be born. They maintain that a woman will suffer more harm if she is forced to have an unwanted child. Linked to this argument is their belief that children should be born to parents who want and love them.

Miracle Babies

On June 16, 1985, in Florida, Kenya King was born twenty-one weeks into her mother's pregnancy. She was over four months premature and weighed only one pound. Kenya was kept in intensive care, and when she left the hospital with her mother, she weighed 4.5 pounds. Since her birth, more babies have been born before the twenty-two to twenty-four week mark.

The record for the most premature baby to survive is held by James Gill, who was born 128 days prematurely, at twenty-one weeks and five days of gestation, in May 1987. He grew to be a healthy young man who went to college in 2006.

Unwanted babies, they claim, will lead to traumatized mothers, child abuse or neglect, and more children being put into the care of the state.

They also claim that making abortion illegal or socially unacceptable does not make it disappear. In states and countries where abortion is illegal, women who are desperate to end their pregnancy will seek unsafe, illegal methods. Pro-choice campaigns point to the correlation between unsafe abortions and countries where abortion is illegal to say that making abortion illegal does not stop women from having them but increases their health risks when they do.

Teen Pregnancies

A major concern for the pro-choice camp is teenage pregnan-

Anti-abortion activists chanting with graphic posters, New York.

cies, with girls as young as twelve or thirteen giving birth. They believe better sex education and information about contraception and abortion have helped reduce these numbers.

In the United States, the Guttmacher Institute reported about 614,000 pregnancies in 2010 among teenage girls aged fifteen to nineteen, or 57.4 pregnancies per 1,000 women that age. This represents a 51 percent decline from the 1990 peak and a 15 percent decline in just two years. Similarly, teen births declined 44 percent from the peak in 1991, and the teen abortion rate declined 66% between its 1988 peak of 43.5 abortions per 1,000 women and the 2010 rate of 14.7 per 1,000. The Guttmacher Institute stated that the reason for these trends is improved contraceptive use; they did not mention spreading information about abortion as a reason.

Pro-Choice Organizations in the Developing World

International organizations such as the United Nations, the Alliance of Family Planning, and the International Planned Parenthood Federation are concerned about issues in women's reproductive health worldwide. They see several major areas of concern, specific to different regions of the world: the high mortality rates in childbirth; the lack of effective contraception which has accounted for the rapid spread of HIV/AIDS; the high rate of pregnancy among very young women; and the large number of illegal abortions and subsequent statistics of women who suffer the consequences of these.

Both contraception and abortion can be problematic subjects for communities in some cultures in the developing world just as they are for many societies in developed nations. While there is certainly a need to control the spread of sexually transmitted diseases and reduce the rate of illegal abortions, there is also a need to respect various cultural

"Reproductive freedom is critical to a whole range of issues. If we can't take charge of this most personal aspect of our lives, we can't take care of anything. It should not be seen as a privilege or as a benefit, but a fundamental human right."

—Faye Wattleton, former head of Planned Parenthood

taboos, religious teachings, and sexual practices in countries that are most vulnerable to HIV/AIDS and have high rates of illegal abortion.

It is also vital to ensure that "family planning" programs are not part of a more sinister agenda that seeks to control populations by subjecting women to coercive birth control methods, including forced abortions. Respecting women's reproductive rights is an important principle in the pro-choice campaign.

Part of the pro-choice international agenda is devoted to promoting access to safe, legal abortion and to increasing the availability of effective contraception and sex education, which could lower the abortion rates. Certainly, in the past 25 years, modern family-planning methods have reduced abortion rates in some countries by 60 percent. These countries include Russia, Hungary, Chile, Mexico, South Korea, Kazakhstan, and Ukraine. The World Health Organization, however, reports

 ## Illegal, Unsafe Abortions in Africa

In Africa—where most countries have restrictive abortion laws—it is estimated that approximately 6 million abortions are carried out each year, but only 3 percent are performed under safe conditions. Nine percent of all annual maternal deaths—approximately 16,000 a year—in Africa are due to unsafe abortions. Studies indicate that 34 percent of worldwide deaths from unsafe abortions occur in Africa.

A mother and child in Guizhou, China. The country has banned parents from having more than one child in order to control the country's population growth. This law is enforced with compulsory abortion and sterilization.

that 86 percent of all unsafe abortions still happen in the developing world—South and Southeast Asia, sub-Saharan Africa, Latin America, and the Caribbean.

The "Global Gag Rule"

The "Global Gag Rule" was a US government policy enacted in 1984 during the Reagan administration. It was also named the "Mexico City Policy," after a population conference held there. The rule prohibited foreign *non-governmental organizations*

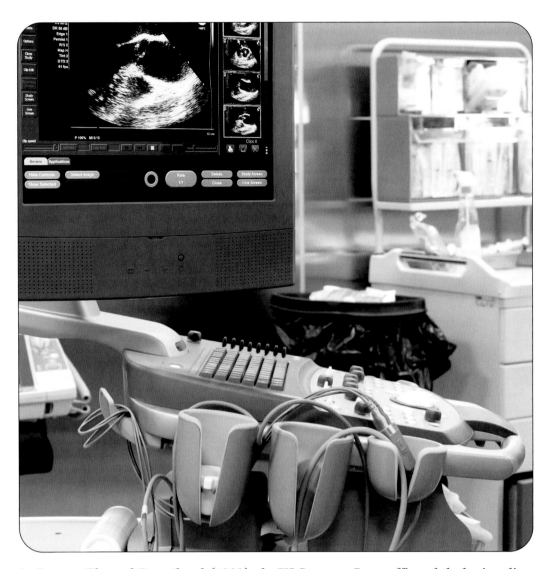

In Casey v. Planned Parenthood *(1992), the US Supreme Court affirmed the basic ruling of Roe v. Wade that the government is prohibited from banning most abortions. However, the Court also ruled in* Casey *that states may regulate abortions as needed to protect the health of the mother and the life of the fetus, and that states may outlaw abortions of "viable" fetuses—those that, if born early, could live outside the womb. Consequently, since this ruling some states have attempted to reduce the availability of abortion by imposing waiting periods, requirements for minors to consult with parents before having an abortion, and rules that regulate how medical clinics that provide abortions are staffed and managed.*

(NGOs) that received US funds from speaking about abortion, providing legal abortion services, or advising people on where to get an abortion. The policy only allowed for exemptions in the cases of rape, incest, and the life of the mother. The rule has been repealed and reinstituted multiple times by presidents from opposing political parties since Reagan's term and is currently repealed.

The Pro-Life Movement and the Beginning of Life

The foundation of the pro-life argument is that life begins in the womb, and many say specifically at conception, the moment when the fertilized egg begins to develop as a separate and unique human being with a full genetic code necessary to develop into a functioning, living being.

Pro-life advocates say the different stages of pregnancy show increasing development of a human being who has the fundamental right to live. The National Institutes of Health explain that the forty weeks of a full-term pregnancy are marked by the following milestones: By week five, the embryo's cells differentiate into blood, kidney, and nerve cells, and the brain, spinal cord, and heart develop; by weeks six to seven, there is a regular heartbeat; by week ten, all essential organs have begun to grow, and the embryo is now considered a fetus. By weeks fifteen to eighteen, the fetus can move and stretch with a well-formed face; by weeks nineteen to twenty-one, the fetus can hear and swallow, and quickening occurs, when the mother can feel the fetus move; by week twenty-six, the fetus can be startled by loud noises, all parts of the eyes are formed, and air sacs start to fill the lungs.

The Right to Life

Of all the major issues facing the world today, human rights is one of the most important. They were first listed in an international charter drawn up by the United Nations in 1948 which guarantees basic rights for all men, women, and children. There are now several charters and covenants in existence that protect human rights globally. One of the fundamental principles written in all of these documents is an article stating that every individual has the right to life: "Everyone has the right to life, liberty, and security of person."

Pro-life groups claim that abortion compromises this fundamental right to life that is due every human being, including a fetus. They cite the World Medical Association's 1948 Declaration of Geneva, which contains a reformulation of the ancient Hippocratic Oath: "I will maintain the utmost respect for human life, from the time of conception." While pro-life supporters acknowledge that the mother's body and life will be affected by having a baby, they consider each life to have equal value, regardless of age. In considering abortion, when comparing the life or death of one person (the child) with the physical, practical, and financial changes for the other person (the mother), the right to life for the baby is of greater importance than the preferences of the mother.

Religious Views on the Right to Life

Many religions of different cultures support the basic tenet that an unborn fetus has a right to life. These diverse views vary in their degrees of tolerance toward abortion. Certain orthodox Jewish groups, for instance, are strictly pro-life. There are also various denominations in the Christian faith that are actively

The Drop Box

Pro-life groups protest against abortion on grounds of fetal abnormality, since they believe this encourages discrimination against people with special needs. The Society for the Protection of Unborn Children (SPUC) maintains that abortion does not solve the social problems that lead women to seek abortion. Instead, it "undermines the will of society. . . to find humane solutions which do not involve killing a baby." One example in Scotland saw pro-life supporters offer money to women in order to stop them from having abortions.

In Seoul, South Korea, Pastor Lee Jong-rak was leading God's Love Community Church and caring for his son, who has severe disabilities. In 2009, he converted his home into an informal orphanage by creating a drop box on the side of his home where people can leave unwanted babies anonymously. The sign by the box reads, "This is a facility for the protection of life. If you can't take care of your disabled babies, don't throw them away or leave them on the street. Bring them here." Pastor Lee, his wife, and a handful of staff have cared for 383 children, from newborns to three-year-olds, providing medical checks, transferring them to other orphanages, or keeping them in his home. About 120 parents have come back to reclaim their child. Pastor Lee's story has been documented in *The Drop Box* film in 2014.

Roman Catholic Cardinal Thomas Collins of the Archdiocese of Toronto speaks at an anti-abortion rally in Ottawa. The Catholic Church has strongly condemned the practice.

pro-life along with approximately 1,000 conservative faith groups in North America. The Catholic Church says that human life begins at conception, and in 1980, a document was issued by the seven Catholic Archbishops of Great Britain called *Abortion and the Right to Live*, which opposes all practices that degrade human rights and dignity, including abortion.

Psychological Impact of Abortion

Pro-life camps claim that abortion causes psychological trauma to the mother. A 2011 study by the *British Journal of Psychiatry* found that "abortion is associated with moderate to highly increased risks of psychological problems subsequent to the procedure." They reported that of the 164,000 studied who had an abortion, 81 percent had increased risk of mental problems. Women who had an abortion were 34 percent more likely to develop an anxiety disorder, 37 percent more likely to experience depression, 110 percent more likely to abuse alcohol, 220 percent more likely to use marijuana, and 155 percent more likely to commit suicide. The study concluded nearly 10 percent of the problems could be attributed to abortion. The American Psychiatric Association said, to the contrary, that a single abortion in the first trimester does not carry higher risk of mental health issues, but they were uncertain of the impact on women with multiple abortions.

Organizations such as the Pro-Life Action League also express concern that abortion on demand encourages far more casual sex among teenagers. Since no contraceptive is 100 percent effective—and many are in fact *abortifacients*—young people will use abortion as a simple solution to pregnancy.

Pro-Life Views on Exceptional Circumstances

Supporters of the pro-life movement point to the fact that abortion is rarely necessary to save the life of the woman or preserve her health. Similarly, abortions where the woman cited rape as a reason constituted just 1 percent of cases; 0.5 percent for incest.

Very few pro-life groups would outlaw abortion under all conditions, and almost all would permit abortion if continued

> "Adoption was such a positive alternative to abortion, a way to save one life and brighten two more: those of the adoptive parents."
>
> —George W. Bush, *Decision Points*

pregnancy would cause the mother's death. In the case of the mother's life being at risk, many pro-life groups provide for an exception because it is a life-or-death matter for the woman and her fetus, who are weighed equally. When rape and incest are the cause of pregnancy, some allow for abortions, but many say the life of the fetus takes precedence over even the incredibly difficult circumstances of the mother who has been victimized.

Some organizations, such as LIFE in the United Kingdom, while condemning the act of rape, suggest that abortion can produce the same kind of feelings that a woman can feel after having been raped, including feeling vulnerable and experiencing loss. They also see abortion as physically invasive and as potentially damaging as rape. They believe that a new life conceived through rape should not be extinguished through abortion, a further violent act.

> "I think it's important that [*Roe v. Wade*] remain legal for medical reasons and other reasons."
>
> —Laura Bush, former First Lady

LIFE believes that if a raped woman receives support and admiration from people around her, she will be encouraged to continue her pregnancy and may feel emotionally stronger by doing so. The fetus conceived in rape is completely innocent and as valuable a person as any other child, and members of

Adoption is commonly cited as an alternative to abortion.

the organization believe that it can be loved regardless of the violent circumstances of its conception.

Alternatives to Abortion

If a mother cannot cope on her own physically, mentally, emotionally, or economically, there are many options for her baby if she continues on to birth. She can explore parenthood with the father or whoever her current partner may be to share responsibilities and resources. If the father is willing to provide care by himself, that is another possibility. She can also make arrangements for her child to live with other family members—such as grandparents, aunts, or uncles—or close friends; these arrangements can be made legally permanent.

Many childless couples would willingly adopt an unwanted baby, including children born with disabilities. The birthmother can actively participate in selecting a family for her child, even identifying cultural, social, or religious preferences. She can choose to have an open adoption in which she maintains consistent contact with her child and the adoptive family; a semi-open adoption where there is periodic contact through letters or photographs; or a closed adoption that protects the mother's identity and privacy and involves no communication except through a third party. If the woman is willing to continue pregnancy to birth, pro-life supporters suggest many different ways that she can provide a long-term arrangement for her baby without having to raise the child herself, and they say there are resources and finances available to make those options achievable.

3-D Smiles

In 2003, images were published for the first time that seemed to suggest a fetus can smile, blink, and cry at twenty-six weeks. The pictures have sparked off a debate as to whether the apparent "grin" is reflecting an emotional response or whether it is a simple physical reaction.

Some obstetricians believe the state-of-the-art scanning

equipment that produces these 3-D ultrasound images is a major advance. It can help prepare parents for a baby's genetic disorders and even show them that a physical "deformity" in the fetus is actually much less serious than they thought.

 # Text-Dependent Questions

1. Explain three arguments from the pro-choice movement on why abortion should be legal.
2. Provide three reasons why pro-life advocates believe abortion should be outlawed.
3. If a pregnant woman did not want to raise her baby alone or at all, what are three alternatives if she continues pregnancy and gives birth?

 # Research Project

Using the Internet or your school library, research the topic of a fetus's right to life, and answer the following question: "Is the fetus's right to life the most important factor in the abortion debate?"

Some believe that the fetus's right to life is not the most important factor but rather the woman's right to choose what happens to her own body without interference from other people. It is debatable whether a fetus can be considered a full human life, but the mother is without a doubt an independent person who should have the right to make decisions for herself. Her needs and wishes are more important than her unborn fetus's.

Others maintain that fetus has a basic right to life because it is a living human being. Newborn babies are dependent, unable to talk or even crawl, but they are considered as valuable as any adult. The same should be true for a dependent fetus—though it is in the womb, it is a human being, and it should have the basic right to life. The right to life is more fundamental and important than any other, even more than a woman's right to choose what to do with her body.

Write a two-page report, using data you have found in your research to support your conclusion, and present it to your class.

6

Trends in the Abortion Debate

There are varying degrees to which countries permit access to abortion. These conditions are covered generally by seven categories, ranging from countries with the most restrictive laws to those with the most liberal legislation. In this chapter we will look at abortion's legal status on a global level and also consider what factors can affect the rates of abortion.

According to the Center for Reproductive Rights, of the 199 countries studied in 2011, 68 prohibited abortion altogether or allowed it only to save the life of the mother, 58 added exceptions to preserve maternal health, 15 also included socioeconomic reasons as valid for abortion, and 58 had legalized abortion.

In late 2015, Planned Parenthood—a nonprofit organization that provides reproductive health services—became an issue in the Republican Party's presidential primary race due to the release of videos that purported to show members of the organization negotiating the sale of fetal tissue. In response, several Republican candidates urged a ban on federal funding for the organization.

Most Restrictive Regions

According to the Center for Reproductive Rights, 68 nations (25.5 percent of the world's population) have laws that ban abortion entirely or permit it only to save a woman's life. Four nations ban abortion explicitly in all circumstances: Chile, El Salvador, Malta, and Nicaragua. Vatican City, the independent Roman Catholic state within the city of Rome, also outlaws abortion in all cases. Other countries, including Sao Tome and Principe, have bans that can be overridden by certain conditions.

In general, the Global South has restrictive abortion laws, including most countries in Africa, Latin America, the Middle East, and Southern Asia. Exceptions in these regions are Uruguay, South Africa, Zambia, Cambodia, and Vietnam.

Abortion on Demand

Places without abortion restrictions as to reason—only for number of weeks of pregnancy—include 58 countries (39.2 percent of the world's population): all of North America except

 Words to Understand in This Chapter

arson—the illegal burning of a building or other property: the crime of setting fire to something.

correlation—the relationship between things that happen or change together.

referendum—an event in which the people of a county, state, etc., vote for or against a law that deals with a specific issue: a public vote on a particular issue.

Vatican City, an independent state of the Roman Catholic Church inside of Rome, Italy, is a place where all abortions are outlawed.

Mexico, most of Europe, and all of Central and Eastern Asia except South Korea and Japan. These countries generally make up the Global North.

On the whole, the continent of Europe is extremely permissive in its abortion laws. There are still heavy restrictions in only three countries: Ireland, Northern Ireland, and Poland, which are all predominantly Catholic. The Republic of Ireland's abortion policy is very restrictive and only allows abortion to save a woman's life. Irish women now have the right to travel to the United Kingdom for an abortion under some circumstances.

The communist countries Cuba, Vietnam, North Korea, and the People's Republic of China are also included in this group with liberal abortion laws. Even in the most permissive states, however, the laws still impose gestational limits and additional requirements, such as parental consent for young girls. Some countries, such as China, also have specific laws banning abortion on the basis of sex selection.

Abortion Rates Country to Country

Recent studies indicate that abortion rates are no lower in countries where abortion is restricted by law. Consequently, these nations have greater numbers of unsafe, illegal abortions than in regions where abortion is legally available. Surveys also show that both developed and developing countries can have low abortion rates.

 Poland's Legal Reversals

Poland is one of the few European countries with restrictive abortion laws. A woman can have an abortion only in cases of fetal abnormality, risk to the health and life of the mother, or rape or incest. In January 1997, an amended abortion law was introduced that allowed women in difficult living conditions to have abortions. However, these rights to have an abortion on socioeconomic grounds were later cancelled in December 1997. The earlier amendments were declared "illegal," since they violated the constitution's protection of the right to life of the "conceived child."

In 2009, the country of Timor-Leste passed legislation making abortion legal in some cases, but after a month the law was changed, restricting the practice again.

There are a number of factors that account for the significant variations among regions. Worldwide, an estimated 50 percent of unintended pregnancies end in abortion. This proportion is slightly higher in the developed world (54 percent) than in the developing world (49 percent). The overall figures range from a high of 77 percent in Eastern Europe to a low of 22 percent in southern Africa. By region, the lowest abortion rates are found in Western Europe. A survey in 2008 showed that among countries where abortion is legal, the highest abortion rate—81 in 1,000 women—was found in Azerbijan (Western Europe), while the lowest—5 per 1,000 women—were found in Albania, Croatia, and Uzbekistan.

Reasons for Variation

Scientific studies have indicated that abortion rates are generally higher in societies where small families are desired and where there is low use of effective contraception, combined with a low desire for having children. Relatively low abortion rates are found in regions where there are high levels of effective contraceptive use or where there is a high desire for having children. Research also indicates that US women who use an effective method of contraception are 85 percent less likely to have an abortion than sexually active women who are using no contraceptives at all.

It is clear that, while prohibitive laws do not ensure low abortion rates, neither does a more permissive legislation. International family-planning organizations and pro-choice groups are adamant that an increase in contraceptive availability and proper use significantly reduces abortion rates. Studies in 1997 show that the abortion rates in Bogota, Colombia, and Mexico City fell significantly as contraceptive use doubled over a ten-year period.

In parts of India, a preference for sons has led to an increase in the practice of killing baby girls, although this has been illegal for more than 100 years. The development of sex-determination technology has been used in the practice of aborting female fetuses. India outlawed sex-determination tests during pregnancy in 1996 as ultrasound technology began to spread with a *correlating* decline in the number of girls born.

In extreme circumstances, some countries—notably China—imposed financial penalties or threats of job loss to many couples that had more than one child in order to limit

A pro-life demonstration in Warsaw, Poland. Zycie jest piekne means "life is beautiful."

population growth. This led to heavy pressure for many women to have abortions, though the policy has been raised to two children in 2016.

Current Pro-Life Campaigns

The SPUC has lobbied Parliament in the United Kingdom in opposition to pro-choice groups that seek to liberalize the current UK abortion laws. The SPUC believes that pro-choice groups aim to lower medical standards in abortion practice and therefore endanger the lives of pregnant women. They are particularly against the idea of nonhospital nurses performing nonsurgical abortions using the drug RU-486 with a follow-up dose of prostaglandin.

The Pro-Life Action League, based in Illinois, has ongoing protests outside clinics where they display graphic abortion signs. The League also co-sponsors the annual SpeakOut Illinois Conference, a coalition of pro-life groups.

Pro-Life Activities is another US-based organization founded by US Catholic bishops. They develop education material on abortion, cloning, embryo research, contraception, and stem cell research, all of which they oppose. They also conduct campaigns in Catholic churches and public squares against abortion.

Current Campaigns among Pro-Choice Organizations

The Feminist Majority Foundation is an organization in the United States that runs campaigns nationally and worldwide on issues of human rights, including abortion. They have con-

Floating Abortion Clinics

Women on Waves is a Dutch-founded organization that operates a mobile clinic on a ship. It sails to countries where abortion is illegal at the invitation of local women's organizations. They have also used drones flown from Germany to Poland to drop abortion pills to women. Their policy is to provide safe, legal, and professional abortion procedures. Some people are concerned that this creates controversy by ignoring the rules of other countries.

The Dutch ship **Borndiep** *has carried Women on Waves clinics that provide abortions in foreign ports where it is illegal.*

ducted a ten-year public education campaign to make mifepristone available to women for early abortions. They also petition for "Emergency Contraception over the Counter."

The Pacific Institute for Women's Health implements pro-

Pro-choice activists demonstrate in support of Planned Parenthood in New York City.

grams that support organizations and media campaigns in developing countries where there are high rates of unsafe abortions and HIV/AIDS. They run clinics and centers in Africa, Asia, the Middle East, Latin America, and the US.

Marie Stopes International operates on a national level in the United Kingdom and globally. Their global campaigns have included "Overturning the Global Gag Rule," which was reintroduced by President George W. Bush in January 2001 and repealed by President Barack Obama in 2009.

Some pro-choice groups, such as Marie Stopes, are also members of the Voice for Choice Campaign in the United

Kingdom, which lobbies for abortion laws to be amended so that women can obtain abortion on demand in early stages of pregnancy. It also calls for only one doctor's approval for abortions from 15-24 weeks and for doctors to declare any conscientious objection to performing abortions.

Increasing Global Tolerance for Abortions

In 1994, 179 nations signed the International Conference on Population and Development Programme of Action, committing to the prevention of unsafe abortions. Since the conference, more than 30 countries worldwide have liberalized their abortion laws while only a handful have tightened legal restrictions on abortion.

Switzerland is an example of a country that has introduced more liberal legislation. In October 2002, the Swiss people voted to decriminalize abortion in two *referendums* called to decide whether to liberalize the country's 66-year-old law or to toughen it further. The final results from one referendum showed that 72 percent of voters backed a parliamentary measure to allow abortions within the first 12 weeks of pregnancy. In the other, 82 percent of voters rejected a proposal by anti-abortion groups to toughen Switzerland's already strict abortion laws.

Restrictive Barriers Raised to Prevent Abortions

While the general global trend has been toward liberalizing abortion laws, there has been resistance in some countries. In

> "You cannot have maternal health without reproductive health. And reproductive health includes contraception and family planning and access to legal, safe abortion."
>
> —Hillary Clinton

Poland, the abortion law allowed for more exceptions in early 1997, but less than a year later, those exceptions were repealed. The Polish parliament narrowly rejected a bill that would have introduced an absolute ban on all abortions in 2011.

The National Institutes of Health state that though countries may have legalized abortion, strategies to restrict abortion access have focused on using barriers that limit the availability of abortion services. In the United States and Central and Eastern European countries, there are mandatory counseling requirements, waiting periods, third-party consent and notification requirements, limitations on the range of abortion options, and restrictions on abortion funding.

Currently, twenty-six US states have a waiting period, which is usually 24 hours, and nine states require counseling about the negative mental health consequences of abortion. In 2011, the Russian parliament established a mandatory waiting period for abortions and considered several other procedural barriers to abortion.

Extremist Violence

Picketing from both pro-life and pro-choice groups have been a staple in the United States, especially since the *Roe v. Wade* decision. This is a peaceful exercise of First Amendment rights to the freedom of speech, the press, and peaceful assembly.

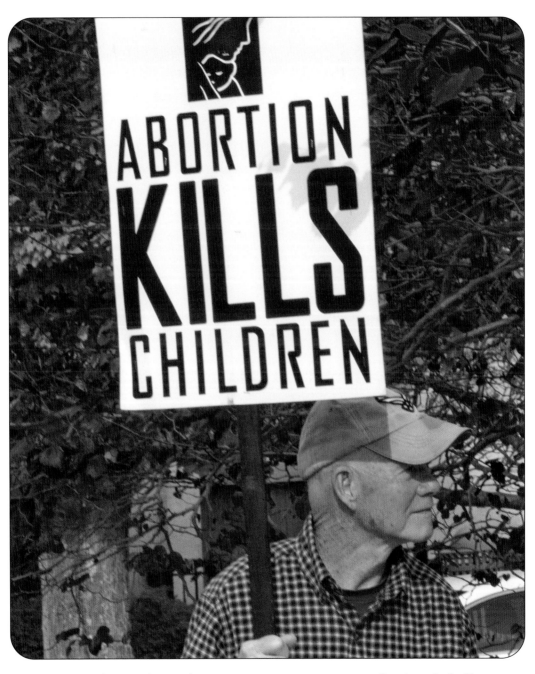

Some pro-life advocates have taken extreme measures to prevent abortions, including attacking doctors and vandalizing clinics.

However, in the 1980s, there was an emergence of violent acts against abortion doctors and clinics, peaking in the 1990s. These included blockades, *arson*, bombing, and murder of abortion providers and clinics by extremist anti-abortion individuals or groups. There have also been incidents of violence the other way—by pro-choice supporters against pro-life advocates in their homes or places of worship.

In response, Congress and President Clinton enacted the Freedom of Access to Clinic Entrances Act (FACE) in 1994. It prohibits the use or threat of force and physical blockade that injures, intimidates, or interferes with a person seeking to obtain or provide an abortion or to exercise the right of religious freedom at a place of religious worship. It also prohibits intentional property damage of a facility providing reproductive health services or a place of religious worship.

> "Listen to the pregnant woman. Value her. She values the life growing inside her. Listen to the pregnant woman, and you cannot help but defend her right to abortion."
>
> —Ayelet Waldman

The Future of Abortion

To an outsider, very little may appear to have changed in the attitudes of both sides of the abortion debate. If anything, it could be argued that the two sides have become even more entrenched in their views. Nevertheless, both movements can claim successes in influencing issues in several countries.

Pro-life groups have increased the attention given to unborn babies and fought for their inherent value as human beings. Pro-choice camps have campaigned for the rights of pregnant women and for the spread of safe abortion options. Perhaps hatred and violence can be avoided if both sides see the benefits the other has introduced, and there can be partnership to find the best practices for both pregnant women and their fetuses.

 ## Text-Dependent Questions

1. Name two ways governments have influenced abortion rates.
2. What conference led to 30 countries liberalizing their abortion laws?

 ## Research Project

Using the Internet or your school library, research the topic of mobile abortion clinics, and answer the following question: "Is it wrong for people from one country to bring abortion access to another country where it is illegal?"

Some think that it is wrong to for people bring abortion across borders because they are not respecting the laws of a country that believes a fetus is a full human life. They are influencing people toward illegal activity, and in the case of drones dropping medications, it is dangerous to send drugs without competent provider care.

Others say that the efforts of mobile abortion clinics are reasonable because they provide safe options that may prevent women from having illegal, unsafe abortions. They also give choice to women and promote their right to decide what they believe is best for themselves.

Write a two-page report, using data you have found in your research to support your conclusion, and present it to your class.

POLITICIANS MAKE
CRAPPY DOCTORS
KEEP YOUR PROMISE
KEEP
Abortion is SAFE
DON'T TRIPLE the WAITING PERIOD

Abortion Statistics

Legal Grounds on Which Abortion Is Permitted in the World

Abortion Policy	% of Countries	% of World Pop.
On request	30 %	42 %
For economic or social reasons	35 %	63 %
Because of fetal impairment	50 %	67 %
In cases of rape or incest	51 %	74 %
To preserve mental health	65 %	76 %
To preserve physical health	68 %	79 %
To save a woman's life	97	99

Source: UN, *World Abortion Policies*, 2013

Legal Grounds on Which Abortion Is Permitted, by Level of Development

Abortion Policy	% of Developed Countries	% of Developing Countries
On request	71%	16%
For economic or social reasons	82%	20%
Because of fetal impairment	86%	38%
In cases of rape or incest	86%	39%
To preserve mental health	86%	58%
To preserve physical health	88%	61%
To save a woman's life	96%	97%

Source: UN, *World Abortion Policies*, 2013

Contraceptive Use, by World Region

Region	% of Married Women, 1990	% of Married Women, 2003
Africa	17%	28%
Asia	57%	68%
Latin America	62%	71%
Europe	66%	68%
North America	71%	72%

Source: Guttmacher Institute, 2009

Abortion Statistics in the US

- Nearly half of pregnancies among American women are unintended, and about four in ten of these are terminated by abortion.
- Twenty-one percent of all pregnancies (excluding miscarriages) end in abortion.
- In 2011, 1.06 million abortions were performed, down 13 percent from 1.21 million in 2008. From 1973 through 2011, nearly 53 million legal abortions occurred.
- Each year, 1.7 percent of women aged 15 to 44 have an abortion. Half have had at least one previous abortion.
- At least half of American women will experience an unintended pregnancy by age 45, and at 2008 abortion rates, one in ten women will have an abortion by age twenty, one in four by age thirty, and three in ten by age 45.
- Eighteen percent of US women obtaining abortions are teenagers; those aged fifteen to seventeen obtain 6 percent of all abortions, eighteen- to nineteen-year-olds obtain 11 percent, and teens younger than 15 obtain 0.4 percent.
- Women in their twenties account for more than half of all abortions: Women aged twenty to twenty-four obtain 33 percent of all abortions, and women aged twenty-five to twenty-nine obtain 24 percent.

Source: Guttmacher Institute,
Induced Abortion in the United States

Organizations to Contact

Pro-Choice Organizations

Feminist Women's Health Center
106 East E Street
Yakima, WA, 98901
www.fwhc.org

NARAL: Pro-Choice California
335 S Van Ness Avenue
San Francisco, CA 94111
www.prochoicecalifornia.org

Planned Parenthood Federation of America
123 William Street
New York, NY 10038
www.plannedparenthood.org

Pro-Life Organizations

National Women's Coalition for Life
PO Box 1553
Oak Park, IL 60304

Feminists for Life
PO Box 320667
Alexandria, VA 22320
www.feministsforlife.org

LIFE
1 Mill St, Leamington Spa
Warwickshire CV31 1ES
UK
http://lifecharity.org.uk

Series Glossary

apartheid—literally meaning "apartness," the political policies of the South African government from 1948 until the early 1990s designed to keep peoples segregated based on their color.

BCE and CE—alternatives to the traditional Western designation of calendar eras, which used the birth of Jesus as a dividing line. BCE stands for "Before the Common Era," and is equivalent to BC ("Before Christ"). Dates labeled CE, or "Common Era," are equivalent to *Anno Domini* (AD, or "the Year of Our Lord").

colony—a country or region ruled by another country.

democracy—a country in which the people can vote to choose those who govern them.

detention center—a place where people claiming asylum and refugee status are held while their case is investigated.

ethnic cleansing—an attempt to rid a country or region of a particular ethnic group. The term was first used to describe the attempt by Serb nationalists to rid Bosnia of Muslims.

house arrest—to be detained in your own home, rather than in prison, under the constant watch of police or other government forces, such as the army.

reformist—a person who wants to improve a country or an institution, such as the police force, by ridding it of abuses or faults.

republic—a country without a king or queen, such as the US.

United Nations—an international organization set up after the end of World War II to promote peace and co-operation throughout the world. Its predecessor was the League of Nations.

UN Security Council—the permanent committee of the United Nations that oversees its peacekeeping operations around the world.

World Bank—an international financial organization, connected to the United Nations. It is the largest source of financial aid to developing countries.

World War I—A war fought in Europe from 1914 to 1918, in which an alliance of nations that included Great Britain, France, Russia, Italy, and the United States defeated the alliance of Germany, Austria-Hungary, the Ottoman Empire, and Bulgaria.

World War II—A war fought in Europe, Africa, and Asia from 1939 to 1945, in which the Allied Powers (the United States, Great Britain, France, the Soviet Union, and China) worked together to defeat the Axis Powers (Germany, Italy, and Japan).

Further Reading

Erdreich, Sarah. *Generation Roe: Inside the Future of the Pro-Choice Movement.* New York: Seven Stories Press, 2013.

Fisher, Brian E. *Abortion: The Ultimate Exploitation of Women.* New York: Morgan James Publishing, 2013.

Grady, John. *Abortion: Yes or No?* Charlotte, NC: TAN Books, 2015.

Johnson, Abby. *The Walls Are Talking: Former Abortion Clinic Workers Tell Their Stories.* San Francisco: Ignatius Press, 2016.

Pollitt, Katha. *Pro: Reclaiming Abortion Rights.* New York: Picador, 2014.

Internet Resources

Pro-Life Websites

www.nrlc.org
>   National Right to Life deals with many pro-life causes but concentrates on abortion matters.

www.feministsforlife.org
>   Feminists for Life of America is pro-woman and pro-life, dedicated to systematically eliminating the root causes that drive women to abortion—primarily lack of practical resources and support—through holistic, woman-centered solutions.

http://lifecharity.org.uk
>   LIFE is the largest pro-life organization in the UK, combining advocacy and education with a nationwide care service. They support anyone facing a crisis pregnancy, pregnancy loss, or after-effects of an abortion.

http://prolifeaction.org
>   The Pro-Life Action League aims to save unborn children through non-violent direct action, including public protests, promoting activism, and youth outreach.

Pro-Choice Websites

www.plannedparenthood.org

Planned Parenthood has information on abortion—
how to decide whether abortion is right for you,
descriptions of the procedures and risks, and supporting information for friends, parents, or partners of a
woman seeking abortion.

www.reproductiverights.org

The Center for Reproductive Rights uses the law to
advance reproductive freedom as a fundamental
human right that all governments are legally obligated
to protect, respect, and fulfill.

www.guttmacher.org

The Guttmacher Institute is a leading research and
policy organization committed to advancing sexual and
reproductive health and rights in the US and globally.

www.fwhc.org

The Feminist Women's Health Center maintains an
extensive website with information about abortion
procedures, personal stories, and poetry.

---

*Publisher's Note: The websites listed on these pages were active at the time of publica-
tion. The publisher is not responsible for websites that have changed their address or
discontinued operation since the date of publication. The publisher reviews and
updates the websites each time the book is reprinted.*

Index

Numbers in **bold italics** refer to captions.

miscarriage, 8, 10
misoprostol, 40, 45
"morning after pill," 42–43

Netherlands, 5, 12
non-governmental organizations
   (NGOs), 62, 70–71

Obama, Barack, 90

Pacific Institute for Women's
   Health, 89–90
Pius IX (Pope), 17–18
Plan B emergency contraceptive, *42*
   See also contraception
Planned Parenthood, *61*, 67, *81, 90*
Poland, 83, 84, *87*, 91
Posttraumatic Abortion Syndrome
   (PAS), 47
premature babies, 62, 65
   See also viability
pro-choice groups, 13–14, 20, *22*,
   61–65, 86, 88–91, 95
   in the developing world, 67–69
   and teen pregnancies, 65–67
pro-life groups, 13–14, 42–43, 58,
   61–62, 71, 76–79, 88, 94–95
   and psychological impact of
      abortion, 47, 74–75
   and religion, 72–74
   and risks to mother's health,
      75–76
   and *Roe v. Wade*, 23–25
procedures, abortion, 39–42, 45, 75
   See also abortion

rape, 7–8, 12, 45, 53–54, 75, 76–77,
   84
religion, 12, 15, *16*, 17–18, *34*,
   35–37, 55, 72–74, 88
research projects, 25, 37, 49, 59,
   79, 95
Roe No More, 25

Roe v. Wade, 22–25
   See also abortion
Roman Catholicism, 12, *16*, 17–18,
   34, 74, 88
Romans, ancient, 14
RU-486 (mifepristone), *41*, 88, 89

Society for the Protection of
   Unborn Children (SPUC), 73, 88
sterilization, enforced, 17
suction aspiration, 40
   See also procedures, abortion
Switzerland, 91

teen pregnancies, *53*, 65–67, 99
thalidomide, 58
The Drop Box (movie), 73

Uganda, 44, *46*
United Kingdom, 7–10, 20–22, 32,
   46–47, 52, 76, 88, 90–91
   and abortion restrictions,
      18–19, 58–59, 83
United Nations, 72

vacuum aspiration, 40
   See also procedures, abortion
viability, *33*, 35, 62
   See also beginning of life
Voice for Choice Campaign, 90–91
Von Leeuwenhoek, Antonie, 18

Wade, Henry, 23
Waldman, Ayelet, 94
Wattleton, Faye, 67
Women on Waves, 89
women's right movement, 20, *21*
World Health Organization
   (WHO), 11, 43, 68–69

Zacchia, Paolo, 18
Zambia, 12

About the Author

Mike Walters studied English and secondary education at Villanova University in Philadelphia. He has written articles for many publications. This is his first book.